HIGH SPEED TRAINS

Holly Cefrey

Children's Press
A Division of Grolier Publishing
New York / London / Hong Kong / Sydney
Danbury, Connecticut

Book Design: Michael DeLisio
Contributing Editor: Jeri Cipriano

Photo Credits: Cover © Dallas and John Heaton/Corbis; pp. 4, 23 © Robert
Holmes/Corbis; pp. 6, 9, 16 © Corbis; pp. 11, 18 © Michael Maslon Historic
Photographs/Corbis; p. 12 © Hulton-Deutsch Collection/Corbis; p. 20 © Jim
Sugar Photography/Corbis; p. 25 © Roger Ressmeyer/Corbis; p. 26 © Steve
Kaufman/Corbis; pp. 29, 35, 36 © AP/Wide World Photos; p. 30 © Bill
Ross/Corbis; p. 32 © Collin Garrett; Milepost 92½/Corbis; p. 38 © Michael S.
Yamashita/Corbis; p. 41 © AFP/Corbis

Visit Children's Press on the Internet at:
http://publishing.grolier.com

Library of Congress Cataloging-in-Publication Data

Cefrey Holly
  High speed trains/ by Joanne Winne.
    p. cm. — (Built for speed)
  Includes bibliographical references and index.
  Summary: This book discusses the history of trains, the invention of high-speed
    trains and the high-speed train systems of European countries.
  ISBN 0-516-23157-X (lib.) — ISBN 0-516-23260-6 (pbk.)
1. High speed trains—Juvenile literature [1. High speed trains 2. Railroads—Trains]
    I. Title II. Series
  2001
  385' .2—dc21

CONTENTS

INTRODUCTION

Imagine going from one country to another in just a few hours, without ever leaving the ground! You could have breakfast in Paris, France, and lunch in London, England—both on the same day. High-speed trains make this possible. Today, there are high-speed trains all over the world. In the future, high-speed train travel may become part of our everyday lives.

Most normal passenger trains travel less than 100 miles per hour (161 km/h). High-speed trains average around 150 miles per hour (241 km/h). Some go even faster. High-speed trains are the latest and most exciting trains in train history. They make our high-speed lives easier by getting us to places faster. Train travel has come a long way since the first trains were built in the 1800s.

Japan's bullet train was one of the world's first high-speed trains.

RAILROADS BEFORE TRAIN POWER

As early as the Roman Empire (27 B.C.), people used railroads. The Romans cut grooves into bumpy stone paths. They built carts with wheels, which went into the grooves. The grooved tracks smoothly guided the carts along the road.

Today's railroad tracks are more like the mining tracks used in Europe during the 1500s. These mining tracks were raised pieces of wood. Wagon wheels were placed on the wooden rails. Horses or people pulled or pushed the wagons along the railed road. The rails guided the wagon along the road to and from the mines. Eventually, the wooden rails were replaced with cast-iron rails. Cast-iron rails,

This picture shows an early railroad that ran through the Alps.

however, were easily damaged. In the 1870s, cast-iron rails were replaced with much harder steel rails. Modern rails are still made of steel.

THE FIRST TRAINS

The early trains made travel and life easier. During the 1800s, different communities were growing and developing that were far apart from each other. People in rural areas needed supplies such as coal, lumber, or food. The invention of the train made delivering supplies much easier.

Before the use of trains in the 1800s, the fastest form of transportation was the stagecoach. Stagecoaches could carry only a few people at a time. Stagecoaches were pulled by horses and traveled at a speed of about 7 miles per hour (11 km/h).

The first trains were powered by steam engines. These engines had the power to pull more weight for much longer distances than

Early locomotives were used to pull stagecoaches.

horses could, in a shorter amount of time. Trains could carry thousands of pounds of supplies. This power and carrying capacity made trains the best way to transport supplies for long distances.

There are different engines that can power a locomotive. The locomotive of a train is named after whatever type of engine it has. The steam locomotive uses the steam engine. Steam trains have a steam locomotive in front, pulling the rest of the train.

The Steam Engine Age

In 1804, Richard Trevithick invented the steam train in Merthyr Tydfil, South Wales. His steam train looked like a huge barrel sitting on wheels. The barrel held water. A coal fire burned beneath the barrel. When the water boiled into steam, the steam moved a piston back and forth. A bar connected the piston to the wheels. As the piston moved, the wheels turned. Trevithick had created engine power.

Trevithick's first locomotive was able to haul several coal wagons hitched to it. A group of coal miners also could ride. This locomotive train was not as large as later trains because it was used for mining purposes. Carts used in mining operations were narrow so that they could fit into narrow tunnels. The train did a great job hauling coal and miners from deep inside a mine.

Trevithick's train was such a success that other people decided to build steam trains.

The conductor and engineers pose on their steam locomotive in New Philadelphia, Ohio, during the 1930s.

By the 1850s, steam locomotives were used throughout the world. Steam trains were carrying supplies and people to different parts of countries and continents.

Before the mid-1800s, the central part of the United States was a vast wilderness. Railroad workers laid tracks through this wilderness. The trains that ran on these tracks had many stops along their routes. Towns sprang up along the railroad lines wherever the train stopped.

This steam train ran in England between Manchester and Liverpool in the late 1800s.

These small towns soon grew into cities. Trains helped in the development of cities by bringing people and supplies to the wild and rural parts of the United States.

In 1869, the first U.S. transcontinental railway was built. Tracks laid from the east were joined with tracks laid from the west. This railway made it possible to travel from one coast to another. The distance from New York to San

Francisco is more than 3,000 miles (4,828 km). A trip this far could take six months by wagon train. But steam trains made the same trip in six weeks!

Trains of the 1900s

Steam locomotives were not perfect. The steam engines made a great deal of noise and smoke while they were operating. The engines also needed a constant supply of coal and water to operate. Train builders worked to build better steam trains, but they also wanted to find new sources of power. By the end of the 1800s, inventors were working with electricity to power trains. Electric trains replaced steam trains in the early 1900s.

Electric trains were faster, cleaner, quieter, and easier to run than steam trains. Today, electric trains are used in many parts of the world. Electric trains are powered by electricity that runs on either a wire or a third rail. The electricity for the wire or third rail is made by an electrical power plant. The train has contact with the wire or rail, which gives the locomotive electrical power.

Another source of a train's electric power is the diesel engine. Diesel-electric trains were invented in the early 1900s. A diesel-electric train, or diesel for short, runs on electricity. The electricity is provided by an engine that runs on fuel other than coal and water. These first diesel trains were faster than the electric trains of the time. They were also more powerful than steam trains. In 1936, a diesel train called the Zephyr set a long-distance speed record of 83.3 miles per hour (134 km/h). The distance was more than 1,000 miles (1,609 km) on a run from Chicago, Illinois, to Denver, Colorado. Today, diesel trains are less costly to run than electric trains. Diesel trains are still used in areas where it is too expensive to use electric trains.

Running Out of Steam

With the invention of the electric and diesel trains, steam trains were used less and less often. Most electric and diesel trains were faster than steam trains. They could carry more cargo and more passengers. However, some steam trains were capable of high speeds. One such steam train was the Mallard. The Mallard set a speed record of 126 miles per hour (203 km/h) in 1938. The run was on the main line between London, England, and Edinburgh, Scotland. By that time, though, common use of steam trains was nearly done.

Today, steam trains still are used in parts of Asia. They also are used on historical tours in the United States and other parts of the world. Train tours across the United States provide riders with a real sense of the past. Some tours even serve food made from original dining recipes used during the steam train era.

Designing with
SPEED in MIND

Not all high-speed trains are designed in the same way. Each country that uses high-speed trains has its own designs. Every train design has benefited from early train experiences. Early train designs were modified, or changed, to overcome several problems. First, trains needed to be powerful, but quiet. Second, they needed to be able to haul heavy loads, but not break the rails on which they rode. Third, trains needed to be fast, but safe—they should not derail (jump the tracks). Finally, the cost to build trains needed to be affordable so that the cost of travel could be affordable. To solve these problems, trains and train travel have changed over the

This Union Pacific train, from 1955, is an example of a diesel-electric-powered train.

Here, workers are clearing out a tunnel so that tracks can be laid.

years. Years of modifying train designs have led to the invention of high-speed trains.

CHALLENGES OF TRAIN DESIGN

One of the greatest challenges in train travel is in the shape of the land. Earlier trains could not go up steep hills. Tracks were laid around hilly land and mountains. This caused the route to be longer than necessary. To make routes shorter, tunnels were blasted through hills and mountains. Blasting and tunneling were very expensive. The early steam trains also filled tunnels with smoke fumes as they passed through them. This smoke was harmful to human passengers and livestock. High-speed design solved these problems.

The invention of high-speed trains allowed railroads to be built over the natural land. Powerful high-speed trains easily can climb steep land. Their speed made blasting through hills unnecessary. Many rail routes were laid without blasting, tunneling, or making the route longer than necessary. When tunnels were needed, electric and diesel-powered trains did not create dangerous smoke.

Special Rail Tracks

High-speed trains run on their own special tracks that are called dedicated high-speed tracks. These tracks have been made to handle the speed of high-speed trains. Dedicated tracks have long curves that are angled (like a

Railroad workers are doing maintenance work on these train tracks.

banked curve on a racetrack). This design
keeps high-speed trains from tipping over
while going around curves.

Dedicated tracks have special rails, too.
Dedicated rails are welded together end to end
so that there are no spaces between their con-
nections. Dedicated tracks are smooth and
even, which improves the ride.

Older tracks used by regular trains can be
modified for high-speed train use. When high-
speed trains use these older tracks, they must

run at slower speeds. Older tracks have sharp curves or angles that are dangerous for fast-moving trains. Some high-speed trains have been designed to tilt when they ride on modified tracks. Tilting trains take the place of a banked track. This modification allows the train to go faster than normal.

COMMON DESIGN IDEAS

There are some things that all high-speed train designs have in common. A high-speed train needs to be fast, safe, easy to clean and repair, and quiet. It also should be comfortable and affordable for passengers. Designers think about every need when they design the outside, inside, and bottom of high-speed trains.

Outside

The high-speed locomotive has a front that is in the shape of the nose on a jet aircraft. This design helps the train move through the air more easily than ordinary trains. Air pushes against all moving objects, causing resistance. Resistance makes moving objects run slower. This jetlike shape allows a high-speed train to slip through the air with little resistance. With less resistance, a train can go faster without needing as much engine power. When less power is used, operating costs are lower.

Trains moving against air also make noise. This noise can be heard by passengers and by people who live near the train lines. The smoother the shape of the train, the less noise it will make as it moves through air. Designers limit the amount of sharp edges over the entire outside of the high-speed trains.

Inside

Trains traveling more than 100 miles per hour (161 km/h) create air or pressure waves. These waves can cause pain in the human eardrum and have enough power to shatter glass. Making the train cabins airtight has solved this problem. Just as with airplanes,

Cabins on high-speed trains, like this Japanese one, are pressurized and soundproof to give passengers a comfortable ride.

the cabin pressure is controlled from the inside. This way, any harmful pressure waves or loud noises don't affect the passengers. Designers also try to soundproof the cabins, which makes the ride as quiet as possible.

Early train engineers would watch for signals that helped them operate the trains. These signals were colored flags posted by the side of the tracks. The signals warned engineers of track problems ahead. As train speeds got faster, spotting warning flags got harder. The trains went by too fast for the drivers to see and react to the signals in time.

Today, high-speed train engineers ride in cabs designed to give a wide view of the upcoming track area. Huge colored lights hang above the tracks along all routes. Engineers can see these lights from more than a mile away. If a light warns of a problem ahead, engineers have time to stop the train. The trains also are equipped with computer systems that guide and monitor conditions of the ride. The computer also allows controllers at the station to stop the train if there is an emergency.

Bottom

The wheels are an important part of the high-speed train system. A high-speed train has both driving wheels and support wheels. Driving wheels are located in the front of the train, and are turned by engine power. Support wheels carry the train's weight. They allow the rest of the train to move, which is being pulled by the driving wheels. Wheels are held in structures called bogies. Bogies

High-speed trains vibrate because of the contact between the wheels and the rails.

connect two or more pairs of wheels to the train car.

At high speeds, trains vibrate because of the contact between the wheels and the rails. Dedicated rails wear from constant use, heavily loaded trains, and trains running at high speeds. Some design features help reduce this wear on the tracks. The welded rails lessen rail vibrations. Also, high-speed trains are made with lighter materials to reduce damage to the rails.

High Speed Trains of the WORLD

Some countries have high-speed trains that operate within their own train systems. Some high-speed train systems also take passengers from one country to another. Very developed systems allow passengers to use the trains for everyday commuting to work as well as for traveling to another country. The major high-speed train systems and their locations are:

- Shinkansen—Japan
- TGV—France
- Eurostar—London to Paris, or Brussels
- ICE—Germany

SHINKANSEN: THE BULLET TRAIN

Many people believe the Japanese Shinkansen, also called the bullet train, to be the first true

This photo shows the Japanese bullet train making one of its daily trips.

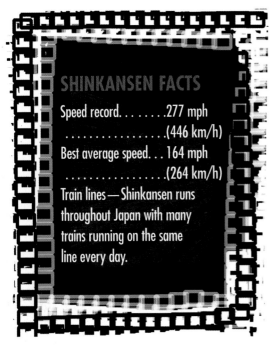

SHINKANSEN FACTS

Speed record. . . . . . . .277 mph
. . . . (446 km/h)
Best average speed. . . 164 mph
. . . . (264 km/h)
Train lines — Shinkansen runs
throughout Japan with many
trains running on the same
line every day.

high-speed train. In the 1950s, Japan wanted to build a fast and convenient form of mass transit. The Shinkansen was their answer. The bullet train started services in 1964. This train reaches speeds of 131 miles per hour (210 km/h). The Shinkansen system runs on dedicated rails and routes. The word *Shinkansen* means "new super express" in Japanese. The hope for the future of Shinkansen is higher speeds. Japanese designers hope to improve the Shinkansen so it will be able to average speeds of 200 miles per hour (322 km/h) or more.

TRAIN À GRANDE VITESSE (TGV)

The TGV is the fastest-running high-speed train. Its trains average 186 miles per hour (299 km/h). The first line was opened between Paris, France, and Lyon, France, in 1981. Hopes for the service were that TGVs would connect Paris to all major French cities. The French company also wanted to connect France to other high-speed services of Europe. Today, TGV high-speed trains run throughout France and in other countries as well.

One popular TGV line is the Thalys route. Thalys high-speed service connects Paris to Brussels, Belgium, and Amsterdam, Holland.

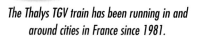

The Thalys TGV train has been running in and around cities in France since 1981.

The Thalys makes twenty trips between Paris and Brussels each day. TGV is scheduled to operate or export trains for services in South Korea, and possibly the United States and Taiwan.

TGV FACTS

Speed record. . . . . . 320 mph (515 km/h)
Best average speed. . .186 mph (299 km/h)
Train lines—TGV train lines run through many parts of Europe.
Countries serviced include Belgium, Britain, Germany, Italy, the Netherlands, and Switzerland.

EUROSTAR

The Eurostar high-speed line is an international success story. Eurostar runs from England to France and Belgium. It connects the three countries' capital cities of London, Paris, and Brussels. The three countries have different electrical power systems, but the trains have been designed to be able to

The Eurostar high-speed train travels back and forth between England, France, and Belgium.

switch between the different systems. When in France, the Eurostar travels at speeds of 186 mph (299 km/h), but travels slower when in England. The trains can carry seven hundred passengers on one trip. The train routes are direct—passengers can board in London and be in Paris within three hours.

A thirty-one-mile tunnel was made specifically for the Eurostar service to England. The tunnel is called the Channel Tunnel, or Chunnel. The Chunnel links Britain with the European continent. The tunnel has three tubes, each with a rail track. Two tracks are for the trains going in each direction, and the third is a service tunnel.

The Chunnel is 31 miles (50 km) long—twenty-three of the thirty-one miles are underwater. The Eurostar system uses TGV-designed trains but is run jointly by British Rail and the French National Railways.

INTERCITY EXPRESS (ICE)

The ICE trains of Germany began service in 1991. Most of the trains run on older, modified tracks at speeds of 125 mph (201 km/h). Some of the trains run on dedicated high-speed tracks at speeds of 174 mph (280 km/h). The ICE train service is used mostly to link German cities. The ICE line also takes passengers into Switzerland.

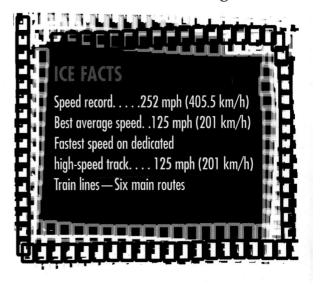

ICE FACTS

Speed record. . . . .252 mph (405.5 km/h)
Best average speed. .125 mph (201 km/h)
Fastest speed on dedicated
high-speed track. . . . 125 mph (201 km/h)
Train lines—Six main routes

The Intercity Express provides train service to different cities in Germany and Switzerland.

The German government is planning more dedicated high-speed lines for the future.

OTHER HIGH-SPEED TRAIN LINES

High-speed trains can be found in other parts of Europe and also in America. The high-speed service in these areas is growing and developing each day. Some countries that use high-speed trains on modified tracks are working to build dedicated tracks and more service lines. Some countries are using high-speed trains for only one or two heavily traveled routes. Countries with high-speed train systems include Italy, Spain, Sweden, Switzerland, the Netherlands, Britain, Belgium, and the United States. Russia, China, Canada, and India also are exploring the world of high-speed train travel.

It is not a surprise if you don't know that the United States has high-speed trains. The high-speed train use in this country is just beginning to develop. High-speed trains are

People tour the prototype of Amtrak's new high-speed train, the Acela Express.

used in California and on the East Coast from New York City to Washington, D.C., and Boston. The train used on the East Coast route is called the Metroliner, which reaches a top speed of 125 mph (201 km/h). By the end of the year 2000, the Metroliner will be entirely replaced by the Acela, which can go as fast as 150 miles per hour (241 km/h). Committees of high-speed train supporters have formed in Texas and California. They hope to bring high-speed train travel to many more places in the United States.

Japan's latest bullet train gets ready for a test run. Behind it is an earlier version of the bullet train.

Ride into the FUTURE

High-speed train travel is becoming more of an everyday way of transportation. High-speed trains are a major answer to crammed highways and auto-exhaust pollution. In some areas, the trains are competing with air travel on an equal level. The future of high-speed electric and diesel-electric trains means more dedicated lines, and more service stops.

THE POWER TO MOVE QUICKLY

Japan and France are now working on new power sources for their high-speed trains. Designers are looking for environmentally friendly power sources that are low in cost and easy to maintain. Experiments in finding new sources have led to new speed records.

In 1999, the Japanese tested a new power unit called the Maglev. Their Maglev train set a world record of 345 miles per hour (555 km/h). Other countries, including the United States, are looking to use Maglev technology in future high-speed train travel.

MAGLEV POWER

Maglev is a shortened combined word for magnetic levitation. The Maglev uses magnetic power to levitate (raise) the train over a rail called a guideway. The levitating height is about 2 centimeters (.8 in.). Magnets are placed in the ground and on the train. The ground and train magnets push against each other, which forces the train to rise up and move forward into motion.

Some Maglev test models use wheels to get the trains to certain speeds before the trains levitate above the guideway. Designers like Maglev trains because they can go as fast as

The Japanese Maglev train runs on magnetic power that raises it above the guideway rail.

today's high-speed electric models. Maglev trains are also extremely quiet, much less expensive to make, and easier to maintain than current high-speed trains.

Because it can travel at speeds of more than 300 miles per hour (483 km/h), the Maglev is closing the speed gap between ground and air travel. Airplanes fly at speeds of 600 miles per hour (965 km/h), and are best for long trips. However, high-speed trains will be used more and more for short trips. The Maglev's speed means that train travel time will be cut in half from what it is now. Imagine—London to Paris in one and a half hours. Maglev technology soon will make that possible.

Here, the Maglev is pulling into a station.

Acela the U.S. high-speed train line run by Amtrak

dedicated track a track designed for a specific purpose

derail to pull away from the rail

diesel locomotive a locomotive that runs on a fueled engine

electric locomotive a locomotive that runs on electricity

engineer a person who operates the train

Eurostar a train system using TGV trains

high-speed trains trains that reach speeds of more than 100 miles per hour (160 km/h)

ICE (Intercity Express) the train system of Germany

levitate to float above the ground

NEW WORDS

locomotive the front of a train that holds the power source

Maglev trains using magnetic levitation as a power source

Metroliner the United States high-speed train line, soon to be replaced

modify to adjust or change

rail a bar that forms a track for the wheels of a train

Shinkansen the Japanese train line

steam locomotive a locomotive that runs on steam power

TGV the train line of France, which serves several countries

tracks iron or steel bars or rails on which wheels are placed

For Further READING

Graham, Ian. *Cars, Bikes, Trains, and Other Land Machines, How Things Work.* New York: Kingfisher Books, 1993.

Stein, Barbara. *The Kids' World Almanac of Transportation: Rockets, Planes, Trains, Cars, Boats and Other Ways to Get There.* New York: Pharos Books, 1991.

Young, Caroline. *Railways and Trains.* Seattle, WA: EDC Publications, 1994.

RESOURCES

Organizations

High Speed Ground Transportation Association—Supertrain Society (HSGTA)
1010 Massachusetts Avenue, N.W., Suite 110
Washington, DC 20001
www.hsgt.org

National Association of Railroad Passengers
900-2nd Street, NE, Suite 308
Washington, DC 20002
www.narprail.org

RESOURCES

20th Century Railroad Club
329 West 18th Street
Suite 902
Chicago, IL 60616
312-829-4500
www.20thCentury.org

Web Sites
Amtrak: *www.amtrak.com*
Eurostar: *www.eurostar.com*
TVG: *www.sncf.fr/indexe.htm*

INDEX

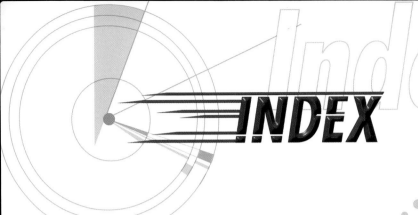

INDEX

About the Author

Holly Cefrey is a freelance writer and researcher. She rode the Shinkansen while traveling through Japan.